a
POLICEMAN'S
notebook

The 1914 notebook of Thomas Smethurst,
a Cheshire policeman

A Policeman's Notebook, 1914 - Thomas Smethurst.

Kindly offered for publication by the Smethurst family, Walkden.

Diary contents © Mrs Lindley of Walkden.

This edition © AURORA PUBLISHING

ISBN: 1 85926 051 9

Distributed by: Aurora Enterprises Ltd.
Unit 9, Bradley Fold Trading Estate,
Radcliffe Moor Road,
Bradley Fold,
BOLTON BL2 6RT
Tel: 0204 370753/2
Fax: 0204 370751

Edited by: Dawn G Robinson-Walsh.

*Printed
and bound by*:   Manchester Free Press,
Unit E3, Longford Trading Estate,
Thomas Street,
Stretford,
Manchester M32 0JT.

> In the lexicon of youth,
> which fate reserves for a bright manhood,
> there is no such word as "Fail".
>
> *Lord Lytton*

Thomas Smethurst

Thomas Smethurst was born in December 1866 at Sugar Field in Farnworth, son of James and Nancy Smethurst. By 1871 the family had moved to Walkden, where James worked as a coal miner in one of the many coal mines in the area.

Improvements in the provision of elementary education by the 1870s, meant that Thomas, unlike his parents, had the opportunity to receive a good basic education. Nevertheless, it was not surprising to find that, by the age of twelve, schooling had finished and work in the mines had begun. By 1881, Thomas, his father and three brothers were all employed in the mines around Walkden. However, Thomas did not envisage a long-term career as a coal miner; and he had received sufficient education for him to consider a career in the police force. This led him to spend two years, between August 1888 & August 1890, as a constable in the Bolton Borough Police; during which time he married Sarah Cooke,

before returning to the Walkden area, where he once again worked in the mines, and also as a furnaceman.

However, he was forced to take stock of life when, sadly, his wife died shortly after the birth of their second son in 1894. He overcame these difficulties in his personal life, to resume his career as a constable, but this time with the Stalybridge Borough Police; where he remained until his retirement in the early 1920s.

Thomas Smethurst in his police uniform

The Police Notebook of Thomas Smethurst

Thomas Smethurst was born in 1866 in Farnworth, Bolton. As a member of the Stalybridge Police Force, Thomas kept a note-book which has been held by his family over the years and is faithfully recreated here. The book has been edited, in order to include the more interesting parts, but forms a reproduction of incidents in the police force in the days when birching was a legitimate punishment, when playing games in the streets on Sundays and letting a chimney set on fire were offences, and when attempted suicide was punishable. The notebook ends with an account of a murder trial, and the emotion when the Judge dons his black cap is still tangible. Many of the offences covered were more minor in character, but sum up the everyday existence of a community policeman in a small town. The recollections are often humorous or sad in view of the characters they bring to light, many affected by drink and poor circumstances.

Some of Thomas's attitudes may strike us as old-fashioned but are in keeping with the age in which he wrote. On occasion, he seems positively humane. Certainly, he could not be accused of political correctness in some of his more judgemental sentiments; yet, he belonged to the days when wayward youths would receive a good telling off from the police, and a march home to their parents. These youngsters were affected by it according to the degree of respect their parents had for authority. His attitudes are often damning but are indicative of the time and help to place the book in context, so have generally been included. In addition, they are not all without some degree of pertinence and interest today.

Many of the incidents may seem to us trivial but it is the over-looking of the trivial which many people now criticise. Certainly, the speed with which minor incidents were dealt with deserve applause compared to the delays of modern court procedures.

Human nature is to be curious about the lives of others. It is always fascinating to peek into someone's diary, particularly when that person has long since died, and their notes are the only reminder of their thoughts and work. It is doubly interesting to peek at the notebook of a professional policeman and to ponder on how law enforcement has changed since the time of his narratives. The book should be of interest to those who love a good story, those interested in local history, to the nostalgic, and to those who are interested in the working life of what would now be a "community policeman" set in the early part of this century. The notebook was completed in 1914.

Dawn G Robinson-Walsh

Contents

Preface

My object in preparing these experiences is to show the reader that, although the routine of a policeman's duty has much sameness, and is rather monotonous at times; yet, it is not altogether void of interesting episodes. He is also in a more or less degree the confidant of all classes of society. Confidences of domestic woes and other matters are reposed into his keeping of which the public know nothing, because for him to reveal them would be a breach of faith, and unjust to the parties concerned.

It is also quite true that in a police-court, every variety of temperament and shade of disposition is depicted. Refinement and vulgarity stand side by side; wit and humour bubble up causing much merriment; smiles and tears are indulged in which excite sympathy; while vindictiveness and cunning vie with each other for supremacy.

There are many people who simply dread a police-court, while for others it seems to have a special fascination. Day by day, these people wend their way to the court, some to satisfy a morbid curiosity by listening to the quarrels of the litigants, and the sordid details of the failings and weaknesses of their fellow-creatures; while others go to listen to the eloquence of counsel in expounding the technicalities and unravelling the intricacies of the law, and the cold, calm reasoning of the learned judge when summing up the evidence submitted to him by counsel, for his consideration and decision.

Such is the disparity in the temperaments and dispositions of people in their likes and dislikes, that one is amazed at the diversity of people's thoughts and ideas; but, on reasoning the matter out one comes to the conclusion; that such divergence is necessary and essential to the progress and advancement of our civilization and the world at large, for if all our thoughts, ideas and opinions were the same, the world would stagnate.   *September 16th, 1914.*

Introduction

A short history of the Police Force will show that there is little resemblance between the policemen of the present day, and the policemen of the past. The Charlies or Watchmen, as they were called one hundred years ago, were old and decrepit men who carried a big mantern in one hand, and in the other a long staff, who sat most of time in cabins at the street corners, and at different periods of the night called out the time and kind of weather it was, something after this manner: "It's past five o'clock and a fine morning" or as the state of the weather might be, and then dropped off to sleep in their cabins again. Sometimes these old men had rather a rough passage and came to grief, for the young bloods of that period used to play pranks on them, and even overturn the cabin with the occupant inside, caring very little what happened, or who suffered, so long as they had their fun and frolic.

At a later period, a more robust body of men were enrolled, called the Bow Street Runners, who for a time did good work, caught many thieves and other prisoners and terrorised the night-hawks who infested the dark nooks and corners of the streets for the purpose of robbery; but, from accounts given of them later, they appeared to have turned their thoughts more on themselves and their pockets than they did on the execution of the law, and so began to deal out justice to suit themselves at the expense of the public and property.

It was left to Sir Robert Peel to sweep away into oblivion the Police Force of his time, and to put in alert, intelligent men, whose business it was to aid and protect the public, and not to retard and oppress them. These men wore swallow-tailed coats with big brass buttons, white trousers, and tall, shiny hats and were called Peelers after their originator. It was his proud boast to say "that behind the uplifted hand of one of my men stands the power of the British

Station". It was a great thing to say, but he believed what he said, and no doubt his ideal was a lofty one. So, from those early pioneers of law and order has evolved and grown the policeman of the present day.

At times there may have been a seeming decline or falling off from the ideal he set up, but today, the police as an organised body was never in a more efficient state, and never stood higher in the estimation of the more thoughtful citizens of this country; and every person of a reasonable turn of mind will recognise and admit that, on the whole we have a most satisfactory police force and that we owe a great deal to them.

If we consider that there are about 50,000 police in this country, we may congratulate ourselves on this fact, that the percentage of what are called "wrong 'uns" is very small indeed. Of course, anyone is liable, even with the best intention, to make mistakes in some way or other, and they are fortunate persons indeed who have never missed the mark. Policemen on the average are not very highly educated, nor at times very clear in expressing themselves and in giving evidence, which is a very important matter in their occupation owing to the weight which is properly attached to police evidence, they cannot be too careful in strictly adhering to the true and plain facts of the case because a deviation from them may pervert the true ends of justice and a serious effect accrue to the person or persons concerned.

We must admit that policemen are better paid than they were formerly but the duties demanded of them are far more trying and exacting. They must be extremely civil, courteous, and obliging, display great tact in their dealings with the public, careful in directing traffic, have strength to deal with drunken ruffians, or stop a runaway horse, possess a fair knowledge of the law, be able to render first-aid; also, to be a street directory and railway timetable. All these multifarious duties the policeman is called upon to perform. The necessities of life are dearer, rents and rates higher, so that taking everything into consideration, they are practically no better off today than they were 25 years ago, but still better results are expected from them.

A short preview of methods of punishment in the past, and those of the present day, will no doubt be of interest to the reader and will afford conclusive proof that punishment for offences now is much more humane than it was formerly, and that the attitude of society has changed towards the criminal. The severity of punishment which sprang from the crude idea of revenge in the past, has given place to the recognition of remedial measures as an essential part of punishment, and a further extension of this reformative work amongst the criminal classes is generally recognised by social reformers.

A pamphlet written one hundred years ago by an early prison reformer describes a visit to a certain Court in the City of London. The day's work was nearly over; standing there in the passage outside the court was a row of youngsters of 13 or 14 years old, just brought before the Sheriff charged with petty theft; they had one and all been sentenced to be hanged. The Sheriff made this curious, peevish explanation after sentencing to be hanged a young urchin of 13 years: "I have never seen a boy cry so much". Today, a sentence like that would ring curiously in our ears, but thank goodness since then we have progressed in order to give the youngsters a chance. A Children's Court has been arranged so that young delinquents may be kept out of the common dock, and from being placed among hardened criminals. We also have the First Offenders Act, which gives power to the Justices to bind them over for short periods to see if they will reform by having a chance, which I believe to be a very good thing, and which, in most cases has the desired effect. I have been deputed to birch young prisoners, but that is now almost a thing of the past. Many eminent men charge "drink" with causing directly and indirectly three fourths of the total of crime, but that is no doubt an extreme statement and I think if we take the calculation of the late Chief Constable of Liverpool of 50%, it would be a fair estimate. The evil is no doubt due to a great extent in allowing the public-house to remain the poor man's only club, his centre of enjoyment, his refuge from squalor and overcrowding, and his palace of light and warmth out of the fog and cold. Various are the causes cited and opinions expressed by different people, but there is not the slightest doubt in my mind that circumstances and environment have a great deal to do with the wretched and miserable lives of the poor and our criminal classes.

Thomas Smethurst

I Rejoin the Service

I have remarked previously that circumstances and environment play a large part in most people's lives, and they played one in mine. I had left the service in disgust, with the intention of never having anything further to do with it and had gone into business, but circumstances occurred over which I had no control; after weighing matters up, I concluded that from the monetary point of view it would be the best thing to rejoin the service. So, on 29th July, 1895, I once more donned the uniform, forsook civilian life and became a member of the Stalybridge Force.

On the following Saturday night, I commenced duty at 9.45pm. Together with an old officer, I sallied forth on to the principal beat of the town, Market Street, which was very rough at that time. We had not been out long before we were called in to a side street to a disturbance of a rather serious nature. We went into a house and there found a woman lying on a couch or old squat, unconscious with a large wound to her head, and her hair matted with blood which was flowing rather freely from the wound. We at once set to work to improve matters, told them to go for a doctor and inquired who had done the job, but as is nearly always usual, the thing had done itself. They were a low class family and all more or less under the influence of drink and had been fighting amongst themselves, such a state of things being almost a weekly occurrence.

The doctor duly arrived, who examined the woman and after stitching up the wound which we had cleared of hair and washed, said that she was in a rather weak state from loss of blood, and it was hard to say how things would turn out. We then took all the particulars we could get and awaited events; these fortunately turned out better than was expected, for in a couple of days she was up again and knocking about as if nothing had happened, so the matter fell through. The saying that a cat has nine lives applies to some of these people, for they seem to have charmed lives, and recover from injuries which to all appearances would end their existence. Still, they come up smiling. Such was my inception into the life of the then busy little town of Stalybridge.

Having had some previous police experience, I soon got the run of the town and it was not many weeks before I was sent on my own. In due course, my first case arrived which was the usual drunk and incapable. He had filled his goblet with sparkling wine, drank deeply, but not wisely and so, like Joe Perkins, having got golly and strong, he had fallen like a general in the gutter, to be picked up by the man in blue and taken to a place of safety, and eventually before the Court to pay for his folly and obtain his liberty.

Since that time, I have had many ups and downs, many happy days and many otherwise. It is not altogether what happens to us in life that matters; it is the way we face it, whether in a half-hearted manner, or with a bold front which means to win or die in the attempt. If we smile at the world, it will smile at us in return, but if we weep we weep alone for time and fortune wait for none. Amidst it all I have enjoyed good health, which is our greatest asset, for it enables us to brush aside the ordinary ills of life and sail along fairly well. It pays to keep fit.

The Three Ps

The parents of these miserable young urchins, PY, PB and PK were of a low type of human being, selfish and ungrateful creatures who only worked at intervals, ate and drank like gluttons, wallowed in their filth and slept like hogs. The gratification of their appetites and passions seemed to be their dominant trait, all other matters being of secondary consideration to them. They brought children into the world, caring very little how they grew up, or what became of them, so that they did not interfere too much with the life they themselves wished to lead. It is no surprise to us who see the everyday life of such a class of people that their children turn into criminals for they are born, reared and steeped up to the life in sordid and filthy environments.

These were allowed to roam where they wished, to go home when they liked, and even when taken to their wretched homes in the small hours of the morning by the police, the only moan made by the parents when roused from their drunken slumbers was that they had looked for them but could not find them, so they had turned the key in the lock and shut out their own flesh and blood in the cold and darkness of the night.

If the youngsters happened to be caught at some depredation, and hauled up before the Court, the parents would attend with crocodile tears and lamentations which we soon got used to and to which we gave scant heed and told them that, instead of the children being before the Court, they ought to be in the dock themselves. Since then, laws have been passed to deal with such cases, and delinquents may now be sent to prison. Such was the teaching and environment of these three boys and I may with truth say that when they were out of their parents' sight, they were also out of their thoughts, those who should have been their greatest protectors from the evils and pitfalls of the world.

One Monday night about two months after joining the service, a report was read that during the weekend two shops had been broken and entered into by thieves. The losses were not very great, which consisted mostly of sweets, some tobacco and a few cakes besides other articles left damaged in the shops and it was considered to be the work of a gang of boys. Some of the old constables named several boys whom they thought likely to have done the jobs, as they had been caught previously at similar offences. A verbal description of them was given and where they lived and we were told to bring them into the office and question them if caught out late.

Being on the top, or Park Beat, mostly on the main road to Ashton, I thought it quite possible to drop across them, and so kept a sharp look out. About 11.30pm, going along Ashton Road, I saw some distance ahead three boys coming towards Stalybridge. I sauntered along leisurely, appearing not to notice them, but on getting near to them I made a grab and caught the biggest, the other two darting away. I questioned him as to his name, where he lived, and why he was out so late and from his evasive answers, I concluded that I was on the right scent and took him to the police office.

On our arrival there the man on reserve duty knew him and said "Hello, Percy, here again" and he hung his head. After questioning him about the shops broken into and where they had spent their time on the Sunday, he admitted they had broken into the shops. Sweets were found in his pockets, and he said they had thrown the tobacco into St. George's Churchyard. I then went to look for the other two in any likely place. I thought they might have crept to their homes to see if they had gone there but they were not to be found. I searched high and low, and at last looking into an old cellar, I found them huddled together as snug as a button, fast asleep. I hauled them out of their nest, took them to the office, charged all three with breaking and entering the two shops, and stealing the articles named which they admitted and were then locked up.

I searched the churchyard but could not find any tobacco, and afterwards during the day took the sweets to the shops, which were identified as part of the stolen property. They were eventually brought before the Court, and having similar offences against them, were each sentenced to six strokes of the birch, to be given by the officer in charge of the case, in the corridor of the cells. The punishment was duly carried out in the presence of the Inspector, and then they were allowed to go home, promising to be better lads in the future. The punishment is sharp and smarts when administered, but a few hours after they would forget all about it and be as ready as ever to commit a similar offence.

A Stolen Letter

As the same trio had occasion to pass through my hands at a later period, I place it here to complete the narrative.

One Monday morning a report was received at the office from T.S. & Sons, Builders & Contractors, that after making enquiries as to the despatch by a firm with whom they had business and delivery by the Postal Authorities of a letter which they had expected to receive containing two Bills of Exchange for £40 & £50 each, they concluded that the letter-box at the yard had been tampered with during Sunday and the letter abstracted by some person or persons and would like the matter sorted if possible.

As the district was on the beat I was detailed to work, I was asked to make enquiries and see what I could do in the matter. In doing so, I came across a woman living near the works who stated that at about 7.15 on Sunday morning, she happened to look through the window and saw three boys loitering about the yard, but thought nothing further about it then. I obtained from her a fair description of the boys and came to the conclusion that the three Ps knew something about the job, so I reported to the Sergeant and looked out for the lads.

Eventually, I came across one of them and questioned him in regard to the letter, but he professed ignorance and said that he was in bed at that time; but I stuck to him and said I should take him to the office and enquire if his statement was true. On seeing that he could not bluff me, he owned up, that they were all three in on the job, and that after opening the letter and seeing what it contained had hidden it in a cellar.

I got the other two later, and then took PB to show me

where he had hidden the letter; there it was sticking between the joints of the slabs. I took him and the letter to the office, charged them with the theft, which they admitted and they were then locked up. When brought up, their previous offences were read out and after due consideration the justices decided to send them to a reformatory until they were sixteen years of age.

Since then, I have had no occasion to interfere with their liberty, and I may in conclusion say that having grown into manhood PH has left this country to try his fortune in some other clime, PB has died and PY has joined the army. Such is the irony of fate and fortune.

Carrbrook Strike

Carrbrook is a village situated about three miles from the town of Stalybridge, and is only very small consisting of some thirty or forty houses. The only industry it contains is a large printworks employing some 1,000 hands, who along with the inhabitants of the village are supplied from the surrounding districts.

The village nestles between two towering hills. The one on the left is called Bucklow Hill, which has on its summit the ruins of an ancient castle or fort. The Winter Hill is on the right, and over its summit you may wend your way to the great reservoirs which supply the town with water.

In the month of November, 1895, the Buckton Vale Printworks, a great hive of industry was a scene of unrest and excitement because the men considered that the remuneration paid for a certain class of work was inadequate. Negotiations took place between the parties but without any satisfactory result. The usual notice was given by the men and on its termination, the employees laid down their tools and emerged from the works into the road. The dense masses of thick black smoke ceased to belch forth from the towering chimneys, the engines ceased to throb and snort, the machinery stood still, the ponderous entrance gates were closed and locked and the works became deserted and silent.

Quietness reigned for several weeks, the pickets thrown out to watch peacefully paraded the space allotted for them to patrol and it seemed as if the game was one of time and patience. However, one day rumour was whispered that the masters were going to import "black-legs" into the works. Then matters assumed a different aspect; the pickets were increased and a vigilant watch kept. Several men were sent from the Company's warehouse at Manchester to the works at Carrbrook which raised the ire of the men and finally caused them to come to grips.

As matters seemed likely to become serious, the police authorities were communicated with and men from the Lancashire and Cheshire counties were drafted into the town and billeted where convenient, some in the Town Hall, and others at public houses. All our section and annual leaves were cancelled and we were notified not to leave our homes and to hold ourselves in readiness for any emergency that might arise.

We were detailed to parade in couples specified distances straight from the Town Hall to the works. Horse-police were requisitioned from Ashton to act in conjunction with our own. A body of men were kept at the Town Hall and at the works for emergencies and at last matters assumed lively proportions, for the workmen were getting exasperated at the turn of events, men being imported into the works who would not work at any other time, given good wages, allowed to do almost as they liked, who spoiled scores of pounds worth of goods through inexperience - we were called upon to protect such men as these. The job was very distasteful to us, but we had it to do. All the same, we were blamed by the men locked out; we were very patient with them and they had our sympathy, but angry men will not listen to reason.

For a time, the black-legs were kept together in the works, but they soon got tired of it and wanted to go home at week-ends, and so it was arranged for them. Each Monday morning, a body of police, foot and horse, went to the station to meet the train coming in and the men were surrounded by us, herded together like sheep, and were escorted in that manner to the works, followed by the crowd yelling, shouting and at times stone-throwing. Similar tactics were observed when they left on Saturdays.

This state of things went on for a time, then in order to bring matters to a climax, the masters had built a number of galvanised iron houses and had beds placed inside. They then engaged a man named Graham Hunter, styled the "Boss Union Smasher", to supply them with all the men they would require. He came riding into town in great style, with a coach and pairs of horses, blowing a horn just as if it was the stage-coach arriving in the town from the distant city. Without doubt, he caused a lot of unpleasantness, for he brought some of the scum from every place where he could find them and a rag, tag and bob-tail lot they were too. Everything was done to make the lock-outs give themselves away, which unfortunately some of them did and had to suffer for their indiscretion.

In due course, several of the imported men got very bold, and decided to go out on their own, went into the public-houses and after having had a few drinks began to chatter about who they were and what they could do. The company did not appear to notice them, although some of them exchanged knowing winks, and so it transpired that on going home they were set upon and severely mauled. They had been warned of the risks they ran, but they only laughed and persisted in doing their own thing, with the above result. Several instances of this kind occurred but the perpetrators were not located and the episodes passed out of the public mind.

Winter had now set in. A heavy fall of snow had taken place and the air was bitter cold. The winds swept down and in places the drifting was three or four feet high. There was nothing to shelter us from the biting cold as we paraded the road and we shivered to the very marrow of our bones. At times, the nights would be still and silent and nothing could be heard but the sound of our footsteps on the frozen ground as we paced to and fro, or the distant barking of a dog at some farm-stead on the hillside. The sky would be clear, the stars twinkled and glittered like diamonds, and the pale moon would shed her light upon the mantle of white. At such times it was pleasant to be on duty, but when the wind howled and whistled, and the snow flakes pelted your face, it was a very thankless job.

One night, around 10pm, a loud noise was heard near to the house of the Magistrate Clerk and it was considered to have been done to frighten him; luckily, two officers were near but unseen, and caught the man who had done it. At Court, he admitted firing a revolver in a field, mainly as a lark not to do anyone harm, but as it was done less than 50 feet from the highway, he had committed an offence against the law and was fined £5 and costs.

One Saturday noon while escorting the imports to Millbrook Station, a large crowd gathered and followed us there, and while waiting for the train to come in, someone in the crowd threw a stone which caught one of the horsemen on the top of the head, almost knocking him from his horse, and making a hole in his helmet. A rush was made in the direction from which the stone came but the culprit was not located. He was eventually discovered and fined £20 costs.

Various ruses had to be adopted in order to evade the pushes of the crowd who had now become very menacing, the strike having extended to about its sixteenth week, and the people were really getting out of bounds, but we did no more than was absolutely necessary to protect ourselves from injury.

This incident might have had a serious result, but

fortunately it ended in nothing worse than a good shaking and a roll in the mud. We had got about eight of the imports in a covered conveyance one day and thought we could smuggle them through a new route and so outwit the pickets. Everything was kept quiet until the last moment, then the order was given, the gates thrown open and out rushed horsemen in the front, the vehicle in the centre, and horsemen in the rear; we followed on foot for a short distance and we were then left behind after getting clear of the crowd which seemed to have sprung out of the ground. The cavalcade was on its way up the road at full gallop, making the mud and water splash about by the push of wheels and horses hooves. All seemed to be going on as sweetly and merrily as marriage bells, when suddenly one of the horses made a false step, and fell in the road, throwing its rider headlong into the mud and slush. The cavalcade pursued its gallop, unheeding the fallen horse and rider who were left to pick themselves up as best they could. Fortunately, neither of them were hurt and beyond a shock and a good splashing, neither rider nor horse were any the worse for the adventure.

The most sensational incident occurred one Sunday night. The men had come by train from Manchester and were collected in the police office ready to be escorted up the road to the works. About 20 of us started out with them, some in front and some in the rear. Almost as soon as we emerged into the street, we were assailed by a shower of missiles, but we kept on going. Hurrying on, we arrived at Millbrook where we received another volley of stones, but we continued unheeding them. Arriving at the road end leading up to the works, a crowd of something like 500 people barred the road and stones were freely thrown. Without any hesitation, our staves were drawn, the charge was given and a battle ensued. Blood began to flow and a regular mêlee was in progress when a posse of about 30 police came rushing down from the works into the fray. On their approach, the crowd began to melt like snow in Summer. Over hedges, ditches, and walls they rushed into the open fields, and the ground which ten minutes earlier had been a surging, struggling mass of humanity was left in possession of the police and the wounded who could not get away. Several had severe cuts and bruises but we did what we could for them by bandaging their wounds and those of our own men. One of our men had a severe cut on his upper-lip, others suffered bruises and knocks, and I was no exception for I was black in many places and sore for many days afterwards.

This incident seemed to break the spell for they gradually simmered down and after about five months of play and excitement they went back to work practically on the same terms they had when they came out after their notice terminated.

The Boss Union Smasher after making matters too hot for himself went away, but not in the bold and autocratic style in which he came, with his carriage and pair, blowing his horn, but like a thief in the dead of night, unknown, dishonoured and unsung, or there might have been serious trouble between him and the strikers. Many other incidents occurred which I did not witness.

Since then the place has grown considerably, the galvanised iron houses have been replaced by substantial stone ones, a park has been made, a club built, a cricket field laid and pavilion erected and the village school extended. Cars also run past the bottom of the road leading to the village which today wears an aspect of contentment and prosperity.

A Midnight Scene

The three actors in this drama were the father, mother, and sister of PH mentioned earlier, and as I have given a description of the environs of such families, I will only say that the father was an idle, drunken fellow, and the mother a thief. The sister was a girl of about seventeen years of age, with a prepossessing appearance and skin like alabaster, and it seemed a shame that she should be the offspring of such dissolute and degraded parents.

Chapel Street, the scene of this story, is a street off the main thoroughfare, Market Street, and is close by the Railway Station. It consists on the left of a low beer-house where all sorts and conditions of men reside and a few houses of low type. On the right are a few businesses, warehouses, and an open space at the bottom on which stand the ruins of an old mill.

Shortly after 12 o'clock, one Saturday night, when the revels of the evening were drawing to a close and the town was sinking into slumber, a piercing scream broke upon the stillness of the night and the cry of Murder! Police! fell upon my ears. I at once went to ascertain the cause and was amazed to see two women lying in the street bleeding profusely from wounds. I raised them up, got them into the house and inquired who had done it, and was informed that the father had thrown the kettle at the daughter, striking her on the side of the face making an ugly cut, and that he had struck the mother with the poker on top of the head, making a nasty gash. Blood having run down upon their faces and clothes made them look a terrible sight.

I took them up to the Police Office and the Police Surgeon was sent for, who on his arrival dressed and stitched the wounds and on learning who had committed the assault said he ought to be arrested. The Sergeant and I then went and arrested the half-frenzied madman, caused through drink, took him to the office together with the weapons he had used, charged him with the offence and then placed him in the cell. Knowing what kind of people we had to deal with, we took their statements down in writing, and got them to sign their statements because we knew that on the Monday morning at Court, they would change like the wind and want to wriggle out of it if they could.

Monday morning and he was brought before the Bench, the charge stated, and the evidence gone into and it just turned out as we expected, they wished to shield him and deny what had occurred, but the clerk asked them if the statements which bore their signatures were true, and they admitted it was so, or else they would have committed perjury. I then stated how I found them in the street and brought them to the office, what the Surgeon had done and showed them the weapons with which he had committed the assault.

The Magistrates conferred together and came to the conclusion that the case had been fully proved and sentenced him to three months in each case, to run concurrently, meaning three months in all. Since then I have had no further dealings with them, and believe the parents have left the district. With regard to the sister, the last time I saw her she was married and to all appearances quite happy and comfortable.

Death by Misadventure

A man and a woman fall in love, and eventually marry. In due course, a child is born to them, a fine healthy piece of humanity, who develops into a sturdy lad with blue eyes and light brown hair. It is their only child, their joy and pride, and with his childish prattle and loving smile he fills the parents' cup of happiness. They watch him grow with pleasure from childhood up to manhood, and wishing to help him on in life give him a trade so that on obtaining his majority, he may settle down in life contented and happy.

When that time arrives, alas; a spirit of unrest surges up in his breast, for he desires to see a little of the outside world. He packs up his belongings, counts his money, and taking the blessings of his parents, ventures alone into the great wide world. He goes from place to place and meets with all sorts and conditions of people, some who are friends, and others who pretend to be but alas, are not! He rises and falls with the tide of fortune and eventually finds out that the great wide world is not the same it seemed to him when he was at home. He writes home regularly telling them how he is going on, that all is well, and thus years pass away.

In a weak moment, he gets amongst evil companions and into evil ways, writes only at intervals, forgets the home of his childhood and his loving parents, and finally his letters cease altogether. He becomes a wanderer in the world, lost to parents and friends alone and his whereabouts unknown, until they are notified by the police of his sad and untimely end.

It was one cold, damp, cheerless night in winter that I

went on duty, and although it was only ten o'clock the streets were practically deserted. Here and there might be seen solitary individuals muffled up to the throat, hurrying along the street seeking the shelter of their homes and a comfortable fireside. Even the lights in the shop windows and public-houses fitfully glittered as if they also wished to retire for the night.

I then commenced to work, peering into nooks and corners, entries and doorways to see what I could find. I had been thus engaged for some time and thought that before going into supper at 1.20am, I would just visit a chemist's warehouse leading down some steps to the edge of the riverside to see that all was secure. I tripped down the steps and was surprised to find the body of a man huddled in a heap at the bottom. I cannot say that I was not startled because that would not be true, for the peculiar sensation which passes through a person's system when coming into contact with a dead body under such circumstances and in the dead of night, cannot be imagined or known only by those who have gone through the ordeal, but I can assure you that it was not a pleasant sensation.

I pulled myself together, turned the man over and felt at his face which was icy cold, then loosened his clothing and felt his heart which had stopped its beating for ever. On further examination, I found a large wound at the base of the skull in which I could easily have placed three fingers.

Knowing that the PC on Castle Hall beat would be coming down Melbourne Street to his supper, I ran up the steps and gave a short chirp with my whistle which he answered by turning on his light. He came and asked what was the matter, and on telling him that I had found a dead body, he exclaimed "Nay, tha' never has". On seeing the dead body, he fetched the ambulance, carried the body up the steps on to the stretcher and conveyed it to the mortuary. He stripped the body which was that of a man of about 35 years of age, well built, in fairly good condition, blue eyes, fresh, clear complexion and light brown hair and moustache.

We made an inventory of his belongings, took a description of his dress, and of the body, washed it, covered it with a white sheet and then left the corpse. Next morning notes were sent out to the surrounding districts with full particulars and in two days, he was owned by the people of Manchester. They said he was a cooper by trade and had travelled from place to place for many years, and that they had no knowledge of his whereabouts until seeing a police notice giving a description. On going to the mortuary to view the body, it turned out to be the son mentioned at the start of the story.

The place where the body was found is private and a bridge covers half of the opening by which means goods are conveyed into the upper rooms of the warehouse. The man appeared to have been drunk, and had gone into the opening for convenience thinking it was all level with the street, and must have stepped off the landing, dropped on his head, breaking his neck, thereby causing instant death.

An inquest was held and I related the facts of the case to the Coroner and Jury, who after due consideration brought in a verdict of "death by misadventure" adding that the place was dangerous to the public and suggested that a gate should be placed at the top. The owner was notified by the authorities, and shortly after a gate was attached to prevent any similar accidents occurring in the future.

Pitch and Toss

This game is a source of annoyance at week-ends to the more respectable public which we try to prevent as much as possible; but although gangs of them are frequently caught and fined, the fascination of the game causes them to run the risk in order to indulge in it.

It is also surprising how cute they are, and how easy an officer can be out-witted, even by boys. I was on duty one Sunday afternoon near to a square block of unoccupied houses when I espied in one of the corners a group of boys playing the game, knowing that if I rushed at them from where I was that they would get away. I went round to the bottom side so as to be nearer to them before they discovered my presence. I then made a rush which was so impetuous that I flew sprawling headlong into the midst of them. I made a grab as I fell and caught one, and the others scampered off like rabbits to their burrows. Sticking to the boy I had caught while I picked up the money, I asked him to show me where he lived. Without the slightest hesitation, he took me to a house close by and walked straight in. I, thinking it was his home, let go of him to go and get out my pocket book for the names and addresses of the others. No sooner had I released him than like a flash of lightning he rushed from the house by the back door, which happened to be open, and made off. The inmates asked what was the matter and when I told them laughed and said: "You have been done this time for he doesn't live here." They then told me his name and where he lived.

I went and told his parents what had taken place and asked if he was at home, but he had not arrived. I said that under the circumstances I would not report him for his smartness in outwitting me, but his parents must caution him and warn him that next time I should take him to the Police Office. And so ended that affair.

On another occasion, I had caught one out of a gang of young men playing football in the main thoroughfare on the Sunday afternoon and was verifying their names and addresses when I came across a gang of boys playing the game just round the corner. I caught one by the back of his coat, but before I could get a proper hold of him, he somehow twisted his arms and made off like the wind, leaving his coat in my hands. I stood in amazement at the quick escape, and then made off after him. I caught one of the lesser players who gave the names and addresses of the others, took the coat to the first lad's home and reported them. They were not summoned but warned to attend at the Town Hall where the Chief Constable saw them and admonished them. The young men playing football were summoned and each fined 5 shillings costs.

One Sunday, two of us went out in plain clothes and had rather better luck. We had not been out long before we spotted a gang busy at the game, so we watched them for a few minutes and then arranged for a capture. He went to the rear of them and drove them towards where I was waiting. I made a grab and caught one with money in his hand, and my mate also caught one. We took them to the Police Office, got all their names and addresses, verified them, allowed the youths to go home, and told them they would all be reported.

We then went on to the other side of town and were casually walking when we saw two playing on the footpath which runs through the fields. We watched them for a few minutes and then caught one each. Although caught in the act, they protested and said they were doing nothing, so we took them home and reported them. We caught seven that day who were each fined 5 shillings and costs, so that it was not a bad afternoon's work we had done that day.

These few cases will be sufficient to show that, particularly in the Summer months on a Sunday afternoon, it is a very common practice in many parts of the town. To eradicate it altogether would be a very difficult matter, but we do our best in trying to prevent the rising youths coming under its wicked influence.

An Early Visitor

In the early part of my career it used to be a common occurrence for all the men leaving duty at 2am to sit and chat for half an hour or so nearly every morning. The "esprit-de-corps", or comradeship was more unanimous then than it is today, for they worked more together as a collective body. Now, individualism is rampant, in consequence of the influx of so much new blood, and the spirit of power is the dominant factor because they are nearly all obsessed with the idea to become superiors before they have become good policemen. Such is the spirit which pervades the Service at present, and some of them are so void of principle and consideration for their comrades that they will stoop to any mean action in order to gain their object and secure promotion.

It was one morning when leaving duty at 2am that this incident occurred. We were sitting chatting as usual after being dismissed. I was sitting on the edge of the table which gave me a view straight across the office and into the street. One of the men was telling a story and I turned my face towards the speaker. It was only for a moment, but when I looked again in the direction of the door, my gaze fell upon the most frightful object I ever saw in human shape. There, standing in the middle of the office floor was a woman in a nude state. This was the most grotesque figure I have ever seen as she stood there with uplifted hands, dishevelled hair which flowed over her shoulders, a disjointed hip, great round eyes which seemed to be starting from their sockets, covered with blood almost from head to foot.

Seeing my look of astonishment, the conversation ceased and every man started to his feet to look at what I was pointing, and then made a rush towards the woman. I asked "what is the matter?", and she replied "Oh, don't let them touch me, keep them off, they are following me". We then saw that the woman was demented. The Sergeant and the other men took her into the corridor of the cells, covered her with rugs and placed her on the couch, while I telephoned the doctor who upon examining her said that she must be conveyed at once to hospital.

A man was despatched for her relatives and clothes, and I was sent for a cab. I drove her and her friends to the hospital where she was temporarily detained for three days. She was eventually removed to Parkside Asylum, Macclesfield, where she remained for several months and died there, never recovering from the shock she received that night.

It appears that she had been very religious and was really suffering from religious mania which had unhinged her, causing her to open the bedroom window and throw herself on to the street. What struck me very forcibly was how she escaped being killed outright by such a fall, but despite it, she had walked afterwards nearly half a mile in that nude state on the cold pavement to the police office.

A Would-Be Suicide

The bridge which spans the River Tame at the bottom of Mottram Road is a strong, stone structure which connects Lancashire and Cheshire and is an old landmark of the town, having been in existence since 1721. On the right of it near to the end of the bridge stands an old fashioned house which was built in 1728, bearing the name of "Bohemia" with its garden of flowers in front. From an old picture of the house, I have seen, it must have been a very beautiful spot. A little further on stands an old church and graveyard, which, in the flood of 1872 was undermined by the rush of water causing one portion of the yard to subside and carry with it several of the coffins into the river. At the same time, a wooden bridge a little further up was wrenched from its foundation while a man with his horse and cart were on it, and all were caught in the surging current. The man was saved from a watery grave but the horse was drowned and afterwards was recovered lower down the river. On the other side of the bridge near the edge of the old Roman road stands the old "Pack Horse Inn" where it is said that in former times when body-snatching was in vogue, the thieves used to meet together and make their plans to carry out their wicked and contemptible trade of the dead.

Many strange things have happened since its erection. One Friday night, the clock in the Market Tower was just chiming the hour of 11pm as I stood on the river bridge. There were very few people about although the night was nice and warm. While thus standing, I saw a man leaning on the wall on the opposite side of the bridge, and could hear him mumbling to himself, but could not make out what he said. I knew the man quite well and could see he was the worse for drink and appeared to be in trouble. He told me that things were in a bad way, he had got to the end of his resources and was intending to drop into the river out of the way and end it all.

I told him he must not talk in that manner and advised him to pull himself together and go home to his wife and children and that he would be better and think differently in the morning. I then moved away a few steps and on looking back was surprised to see him climbing the parapet to drop into the river. I rushed back and just grasped his arm as he was going over, and throwing all my weight on it prevented him going any further. Gradually working myself over the wall with my left hand, I gripped him by the trousers and hauled him back on to the footway. He kept asking me to let him drop into the river out of the way. Had he been a heavy man, it would have been impossible for me to pull him back from the position in which he had placed himself.

I took him to the Police Office, charged him with the offence and he was locked up. I went to his home and informed his wife who was waiting for him, and told her to be at Court the following morning. He was brought up before the Court and was then very penitent, saying that he was sorry and that he would not attempt any such thing again. He had been drinking and he was in financial difficulties, causing him to feel depressed, so had determined to end it all. The Bench bound him over on good behaviour and allowed him to go home.

The Chairman complemented me on my prompt action and said that the man owed his life to me, for without any doubt if he had dropped into the river he would either have been poisoned by the filthy water or have suffocated from the slush and dirt, and that he ought to be very thankful that I was at hand to prevent him from committing the cowardly and foolish act. He has now left the town to try his luck in some other district away from his former associates and false friends.

Horace, Thomas and Harold Smethurst

A Wasted Life

Born of well to do parents, of robust health and good appearance, blessed with brilliant gifts, facilities ever at his command, trained as an architect and surveyor, with prospects of the brightest, the subject of this story might have risen high in his profession and become a leading light.

All went well with him for some time and eventually he got married. His home was beautifully furnished, his wife a good and lovely woman and they were, in due course, blessed with an only child, a daughter. It seemed as if his life would be one long summer day.

Alas, a change took place in this happy homestead, for his wife, whom he passionately loved, was stricken down and taken from his side. His grief was keen, but for the sake of his child, he bore his lot with fortitude. Then, as if that blow was not sufficient, his child was also taken and he was left to grieve in silent solitude. He brooded in secret, became silent and reserved and somewhat defiant of the world, mixed but little in society and eventually refused invitations and busied himself with his sorrow in the solitude of his home.

His sorrow had bowed him down, and solitude and reflection had plunged him into a dull apathy of despair, causing him to lead a kind of mechanical existence. Life seemed but a dreary road, which no gleam of hope could brighten.

After a time, he roused from his stupor, mixed with boon companions and took to drink to drown his sorrows. For years he roamed about working and drinking, gradually sinking down and down into his slough of despondency and disaster until at last he became an inhabitant of the common lodging house and mixed with the lowest dregs of society. At times, he took his meals at the coffee houses where they, out of pity, used to let him stay for hours.

One night, while at the rear of some houses, I heard a noise and found him sitting on a seat half perished with cold. I took him to the Police Office where he was allowed to stay for pity's sake and when morning dawned, he was sent about his business. Lower and lower he descended into his degradation, disowned by his family, friends and acquaintances, lost to all sense of shame and a horror to himself. One morning, his lifeless body was found lying in his bed at the lodging house. We were notified and took the body to the mortuary. An inquest was held and the verdict given was "death caused by neglect, accelerated by drink".

The funeral preparations were arranged by his relatives and the body was deposited in the churchyard, in a drunkard's grave. Ruined, neglected, forsaken and a wreck, he had simply fulfilled the destiny which he had carved out for himself by his own hand.

Heavily Fined

The landlord of this beer house had been suspected for a considerable time of contravening the licensing laws and having received certain information from outside sources, a strict watch was kept on the premises.

One Sunday night, I was on duty in the vicinity of this house, and on seeing a light burning at 12.45am, I went to see what was the reason. I went to the door and listened, hearing a man say "Who pays for the next drinks? I paid for the last one". I mentioned to the Sergeant the conversation I had heard and together we listened to the conversation for a few minutes longer, then knocked on the door and were admitted.

In the living part of the house were the landlord and two other men. There were four glasses on the table, three of them empty and the other half full of beer. We asked the landlord how he accounted for the two men being there at that time in the morning and he replied that one was a waiter and the other a lodger. We left, but I was not satisfied with his answer and waited to see if anything turned up. I had not been waiting long when I saw someone leave the house and dart through an entry close by. I met him full in the face and saw it was the man I suspected did not live there. I went along the street with him and saw him open the door of a lodging-house, so asked if he lived there. He replied "find it out", went in and shut the door. The Sergeant and I visited the beer house, knocked up the landlord and asked him why he had given us a false explanation on our previous visit. He seemed in a terribly nervous state and in a halting tone said "I am very sorry; I hope you will let it go by". We then told him he would be reported and left the house.

A week later, a case came on for hearing before a full bench of magistrates where I gave evidence, corroborated by the Sergeant. The deputy of the lodging house was also called as a witness and stated that he knew the man very well, that he lived at their lodging house and slept in the same room as himself.

The solicitor for the defence said that his client absolutely denied the charge brought against him. On that particular Sunday this man went to his house and made arrangements to lodge there. This would be proved by two independent witnesses. It was arranged that the man should go there that night. He did not, however, go until four o'clock in the afternoon and the landlord grumbled at him and said he should have been in before that time. They had some bother about it, and were still bothering when the officers came on the scene. Nothing more would have been said had it not been for the foolish act of the supposed lodger who being slightly inebriated after some words with the landlord got up and went out saying that he would go and sleep where he would and not be grumbled at by the landlord and watched by the police. There was no drink sold after 10 o'clock that night. The landlord had been at the house for three years, had always tried to conduct it properly and there was no previous conviction against him. He came to Stalybridge with excellent testimonials and asked the bench when they had heard the defence to dismiss the case.

The evidence went on. The bench adjourned for fifteen minutes and their unanimous opinion was that the charge had been fully proved of being open during prohibited hours. The landlord would be fined £5 and costs but the licence would not be endorsed. The charge against the waiter was withdrawn, but the lodger was charged with being on the premises for an unlawful purpose and fined 10 shillings and costs or 14 days. The proceedings lasted for at least three hours and excited a great deal of interest.

A Street Scene

One Saturday night at about ten minutes to eleven, I was standing near to the White House Hotel in Market Street when I received a complaint from a man of having been shamefully insulted by a man whom he pointed out to me.

On going towards the accused, he commenced to run, so I gave chase and caught him at the bottom of the street. A large crowd immediately gathered round to see all the fun. I asked him what he had been doing, but he refused to answer, and lifted up his fist to strike me in the face. Seeing his intention, I caught his arm, pushed my knee into his stomach and held him against the wall. We had a violent struggle and went down in the street, but I eventually got him handcuffed. He refused to get up and kicked and plunged like someone mad. Another officer came on the scene and after much trouble we got him to the Office. During the scuffle, he somehow tripped me, causing me to fall with my leg in an awkward position, with the result that the muscle of my right leg was badly sprained and was black and very painful for many days.

On the Monday morning, his excuse was that he had only been back from India a few days and having had a drink or two, it must have got hold of him for he lost his senses and did not know what had occurred. If they would overlook it, he would go straight in future. The Chairman said that they would have been inclined to deal leniently with him, but he had a bad record, although it was some years since he was before the court. He would be fined 5 shillings and costs or 14 days.

Amusing Dialogue in Court

Much amusement was caused in court one day by an old woman who was charged with firing her house chimney. A trifling thing, but still it is an offence.

When charged she replied:

"No, it never was, and it only smoked".

On my going into the box to prove the case, it caused her to exclaim:

"Is that the policeman?"

I stated that at about 1.20 on Friday afternoon, I was in Quay Street when she interrupted me and said:

"I am a bit deaf! What does he say?"

I crossed the Court to where she was standing and in a loud voice said that her chimney had been on fire.

Woman: "It was not and the neighbours can tell you different".

I: "I called your attention to it. There was burning soot falling into the fire. I asked you how it had occurred and you said that you had gathered some shavings and thrown them on the fire".

Woman: "I told you, I had brought them out of the bedroom".

I: "I asked you how long it was since it was swept and you said twelve months".

Woman: "Well, it was not on fire when you saw it. The neighbours can tell you it was not on fire. I had just been sweeping the bedroom and a few shavings and dust I gathered up, I just threw on

	the fire. They can tell you that it didn't blaze".
The Mayor:	"Have you any neighbours here?"
Woman:	"No, but I could fetch them all up. You know very well it never blazed".

When told she would have to pay 4/6 for costs she exclaimed:

	"Well, I have lived for 72 years and it is the first time I was in a court in my life. How much is it?"
Inspector:	" You have to pay 4/6 for costs".
Woman:	" All right! That's for having the chimney smoking, but I'll fire it next time".

Later, the old woman asked for time to pay the money.

Clerk:	"When can you pay - on Saturday?"
Woman:	"Saturday! Can I thump! Nor th' Saturday after. You will have to take it at so much a week and have missings". She also said that she was living with her daughter.
Mayor:	"You haven't bought her new clothes for Whitsuntide yet, have you?"
Woman:	"No; she has had none this many a year".
Mayor:	"Well, we will give you a week after Whitsuntide to pay it; that's three weeks".
Woman:	"Shall I have to come again then?".
Chief:	"No, we hope not".
Mayor:	"Bring the money to the Police Office".

As she left the box, the defendant began laughing and dancing and, amid laughter left the court exclaiming:

"Oh, heavens protect us".

Slight offences in many cases caused much amusement in court and roars of laughter at the drollery of the defendants when defending themselves. Such incidents lose much of their original humour when put in cold print.

Thomas Smethurst

Stop, Thief!

There is an old saying that "when thieves fall out, honest men get their own" which no doubt has a lot of truth in it, for when they fall out, we generally get to know all we want without asking for it.

On calling in the office one Saturday afternoon, I was told by the Inspector to go to Ashton Town Hall for a man they had in custody, who with another man who had run away, had stolen a barrow and a piece of iron 232lbs in weight belonging to the Corporation.

On arriving there, I asked the prisoner who was his accomplice and where they had been lodging. He told me the man's name and that of the lodging house. Knowing a man of that name, I went to this place.

"Get up, Jim, and put your coat on. I want you". He replied: "Has that b. . . . . . given me away?" I replied "Yes". I then took him to the Ashton Police Office, and on seeing the other man, he said:

"Tha' art a nice b. . . . . . giving me away, but it was thee as planned it and I'll tell tale".

I then brought them to Stalybridge, charged them and they were locked up. They were brought before the court later and after hearing the evidence, the magistrates committed them to Knutsford Quarter Sessions.

One of the men, employed on the "Flatts" saw them wheeling a barrow, containing something covered with a sack. He remonstrated with them, and they put the barrow down, jumped over the wall, ran along the bank into Ashton, followed by this man, and one of them was handed into custody.

They were eventually brought up at the Quarter Sessions, and the one who suggested the theft received nine months, the other three months.

Inn-Keeper Summoned

One Saturday night, I was standing in Market Street at about 9.15pm when I received communication and went to the Blue Bell Inn. Inside the doorway, I found a man and a woman struggling, the landlord being at that time in the bar. On going into the tap-room, I found everything in a state of disorder and all the people in the house more or less drunk and pulling each other about. A man was laid on the floor unconscious and with the assistance of another officer we placed him upon the table and sent for a doctor. Another man was mad drunk and had to be held down forcibly.

The case was duly brought to court and there was a huge concourse of people, the court being packed in all parts available. The solicitor for the prosecution stated the case, describing the interior of the house and also the back passage where a number of steps lead to a tunnel where a man had fallen down.

Mayor: "Was the tunnel lighted?"

Prosecution Solicitor: "I cannot say".

Defence Solicitor: "I can tell you that it was not".

Prosecution Solicitor: "Two Constables went into the Blue Bell and found a man on the floor unconscious. Another man was acting like a raving lunatic, and had to be forcibly held down by the police, and finally locked up. He was brought up and fined, pleading guilty".

Defence Solicitor: "I object to this thing being mentioned as it is unfair to the licensee".

Prosecution Solicitor: "I am simply stating a fact; he was charged and pleaded guilty".

Defence Solicitor: "Again I protest and most strongly. I

have seen the man who says he was not drunk and the reason he pleaded guilty was in order that he might be more leniently dealt with."

I was then called and cross-examined by the Solicitor for the Defence who asked me why I went to the house. Would I swear that all the people in the house were drunk? Did the Blue Bell do its share of business? Did I think that the man was drunk or had only fainted?

I replied that I should not have gone to the house without being called, I would not swear that they were all drunk, but that they were all more or less under the influence of drink, that I did think the Blue Bell did its share of business, that the fall down the steps no doubt had made the man sick but I believed he had had a lot to drink. My evidence was corroborated by PC Lawton, Sgt. Lee, Sgt. Hobson and PC Beever. When Sgt. Hobson was giving evidence there was a tiff between the Mayor and the Prosecution Solicitor:

Solicitor: "The Sergeant said the man whom the police were holding down was mad drunk".

Mayor: "Probably excited?"

Hobson: "No Sir, he was drunk".

Mayor: "How could you tell if he was on the floor? He might have only been excited?"

Solicitor: "Might I suggest that you should not lead the witness?"

Mayor: "I shall ask the witness what questions I like!"

PC Beever, in answer to questioning: ". . a man was not drunk if he was under the influence of drink".

Defence Solicitor: "You have done more this morning to define drunkenness than any lawyer in this country can do, and it will be very useful for me to quote later on".

A civilian was then called who stated that he was a customer at the Blue Bell that night, and all the people in the house on that night were more or less drunk. The man who had been sick and the other who had been locked up were both drunk.

Prosecution Solicitor: "What do you base that on?"

Witness: "I turned him over on his side to get the beer out of him"

The man who fell down the steps was next called and said that he and his mate went from pub to pub and then to the Blue Bell but added that he was fit to be served when he went there. The questioning continued.

The other man was then called who had pleaded guilty to being drunk, who said that he only visited one public house in the afternoon, and one in the evening, and if his friend said that they went into half a dozen houses, it was false. From 4 o'clock to 8.30, he had "tonics" and three or four pints of beer. They had a pint at the Blue Bell. He was not drunk, and would have been served by any landlord in the town. In defence, the Solicitor said that his client had an exceedingly good record, and had an excellent character. It was the easiest thing in the world to bring a charge against a publican, no matter how careful he might be in conducting his house. A landlord was only human and could not watch every part and room in his house; moreover, he could not afford to pay someone else to do it, nor could he define whether everyone who entered his house was sober. It had been laid down clearly that if a publican took all reasonable care to prevent drunkenness and did not commit or connive, he could not be held responsible. Were it not so the position of a publican would be intolerable and no man with a grain of commonsense would risk his money in the business.

Marks had only been in the Blue Bell a week and he and his witnesses would swear that the two men left the house quietly and it was after the falling down the steps that the trouble began. The landlord himself sent for the police, and if he had anything to fear, he would not have done that and placed himself in jeopardy. O'Brien saw his friend's face covered with blood ; he lost himself and became hysterical and sank down in a corner of the room. One of the people in the house said to the police as they were ejecting O'Brien: "You are not going to lock him up?" To which the constable replied: "No, I am only taking him outside; he is excited". Therefore, he contended that his client had acted the good Samaritan and should not be convicted.

The landlord when called swore that the two men were sober while in his house, and behaved themselves inside, otherwise he should have ordered them out. After being told that a man had fallen down the steps at the rear of his house, he sent for the police. The man was brought into the house and when O'Brien saw the condition of his friend, he threw up his arms and went into a faint. He had refused to serve the man Tighe whom he thought was not in a fit state to be served.

The Mayor said that the magistrates had come to the decision that, whilst the police were justified in bringing the case to court, they thought the evidence was not sufficiently conclusive to convict. The case was dismissed. I offer no comment; you may draw your own conclusions!

"A Happy New Year, Gentleman"

This was the greeting given to the magistrates one New Year's Day by a woman charged with being drunk and disorderly on the previous evening, a notorious character.

At about 11pm, I was on duty in High Street, near to a place called "The Snug" when I heard that Bridget was on the war path once more. I was suffering from a severe cold and was not in the best of humour. Knowing what a character she is, I thought it best to use fair words if possible, and if she was not to be persuaded, then I was in for a lively time. She seemed to respond.

No sooner had I gone than she returned to the fray and commenced to abuse some people and left, singing and capering about like someone demented. I was fetched again and determined to squash the bother once and for all that night and lock her up. The moment I got hold of her, down she went in the street and tried to pull me with her. I called a man to assist me to take her to the office. He lifted her to her feet and she began to kick, plunge and spit at us, and became very violent before we landed our load.

The language she uses is awful and she foams at the mouth like a mad dog. No one man locks her up himself; it always takes two or else she swarms and climbs all over him. On being brought before the court, she was as lively as a cricket, smiling and bowing to everyone and wished the Magistrates a "Happy New Year". The Chief Constable said that the prisoner had come back to Stalybridge docks after a stormy voyage on the seas of

Oldham where she had about 37 convictions, and she had about 100 convictions against her in Stalybridge.

She then began to tell the usual fairy-tale, that she had two sons who would not do anything towards her maintenance and that she had only come to ask them for a copper or two to help her on. I told the Bench that her two sons were very respectable lads, and that she came when about three parts drunk to annoy them by creating a disturbance which nearly always ended in her being locked up. The Chairman said he wished she would stay in Oldham, we didn't want her in Stalybridge. The prisoner asked to be let go and she would leave the area, but she was sent to prison for one month, and her spirits dropped below zero.

Shop-Door Theft

Parading for duty at 10am one morning, I was told by my Inspector to change my uniform for civvies as a pawnbroker's shop had been broken into during the previous night and a lot of jewellery stolen therefrom. I got a list of the articles missing and commenced my inquiries in the districts of Dukinfield and Hyde. I visited every pawnshop and jewellers that I could find, and left a list for their future reference. In that direction, my efforts were fruitless but before arriving back to the Town Hall, I was able to take something with me.

At about 1.15pm coming down in the car by St. John's Church, Dukinfield Brow, I saw a man with a roll of shirting under his arm walking up the street. Thinking there was something wrong, I left the car and followed the man. I was subsequently joined by a young man who stated that the stuff had been taken from their shop door. I hurried after him and arrested him in Oxford Street, took him to the police office and charged him.

A woman draper and dressmaker identified it as her property and said it was worth 8 shillings. She had placed it along with other articles at the shop door and later in the day someone shouted that a man had stolen something from the door with the result that her nephew gave chase. I happened to be coming in that direction by car so he was caught red-handed.

The prisoner pleaded guilty. He said he was destitute and he had no employment. He had been sleeping out the night before and he wanted to get inside somewhere out of the cold - that was why he stole. He was a native of Ashton under Lyne.

He was committed to prison for fourteen days with hard labour.

Thomas Smethurst and his two sons as young boys, Horace & Harold, who later both became soldiers.

An Annual Report

Perhaps a description of a year's crime in Stalybridge will be of interest, showing the different offences, how many public houses and clubs there are, and how they are conducted. This is the 1912 report.

During this year, 33 persons were apprehended for indictable offences, 113 were apprehended and 191 summoned for non-indictable offences. There have been 55 indictable offences reported and for these 33 persons were proceeded against. Of the 33 proceeded against, 28 were dealt with summarily and 5 were committed for trial.

The total number of robberies reported to the police during the year was 51. The value of property stolen was £52 7s 4d. The value of stolen property recovered by the police was £32 9s 7d. 710 persons were summoned for non-payment of rates, 671 for Borough rates, 19 for Poor rate and 20 for water rate.

During the year 30 clubs were registered. These clubs have a total membership of 5,323 persons or one fifth of the whole population. There are two registered lodging houses in the borough, having a nightly accommodation for 234 lodgers. These houses have been visited twice daily and there is no reason to complain of the way in which they are managed.

The number of inquests during the year was 27.

The police force comprises 1 Chief Constable, 2 Inspectors, 1 Sub Inspector, 4 Sergeants, 24 Constables and one employed by a private firm. Thirty members of the force hold first-aid certificates from the St. John Ambulance Association. Nineteen members of the force hold the Royal Life-Saving Society's medallion or certificate for ability to save life in water. The average number of days of absence through sickness was 1.28 days each. The length of service of the officers and men averages 11 years and 7 months; the average age is 37, with the average height 5ft 10$^{1}/_{2}$".

The force was inspected by Lieutenant Colonel Eden, His Majesty's Inspector of Constabulary, and the usual certificate of efficiency was received from the Home Secretary.

The Fire Brigade consists of 1 Chief Officer, 1 Second Officer and 18 firemen who with two exceptions are connected with the fire station and police office with call bells.

Thirteen fires were attended during the year. The total estimated damage done by fire and water was £22,431 which to a large extent was covered by insurance. The whole of the equipment has been maintained in an efficient state throughout the year.

The Ridgehill Tragedy

This love tragedy took place in a field near the roadside opposite to an old quarry at the top of Ridgehill on the night of May 21st, 1910. The surroundings of this sad occurrence in summer are beautiful. From the top of this hill you can see the borders of four counties: Lancashire, Cheshire, Derbyshire and Yorkshire.

Mossley Road runs along the foot of Ridgehill and I was on this particular beat that night. At 11.45pm, I passed the end of this road where the two men came running down with information of the tragedy. Had I been delayed only five minutes, I should have been the first officer on the scene, for they ran down Cockerhill which I had just come up, and straight into the office to tell the Inspector what they had seen.

He at once ordered the ambulance to be taken up and went with the men to the place. There they found the body of the woman and the man rolling about and groaning from the wound in his throat. The man was at once conveyed to the Infirmary and the body of the woman to the mortuary. I afterwards went with the Inspector to the home of the young woman to inform her family of what had taken place.

Later, I was in charge of the man at the Infirmary until he became convalesced enough to be brought before the court. During this time, he wrote three letters, the originals of which I detained and sent his friends copies of them so that we might be able to identify his handwriting at the trial. He was eventually brought before the court, the evidence submitted, and on his solicitor's advice he pleaded not guilty reserving his defence. He was then committed to take his trial at the Chester Assizes. On the rising of the court, a cab was sent for, and another officer and I conveyed him to Knutsford Gaol to await his trial on 14th July, 1910.

The Prosecutors for the Crown at the Assizes were Mr. Ellis Griffiths, MP, and Mr. Marshall. The prisoner was defended by a barrister, and a Stalybridge solicitor.

When brought into the dock at Chester Assizes, there was very little difference in Derrick's appearance. He still wore the bandages around his neck, and the wound in his throat which he had self-inflicted seemed a source of trouble. The charge was then read out to him that he did "feloniously and with malice aforethought kill and murder one Hannah Mary Etchells" to which he replied in a firm voice "Not Guilty". He was accommodated with a seat in the dock and throughout the day took a close interest in the proceedings.

The court was crowded, the Barristers' tables were completely filled with wigs and gowns. The twelve good men and true sat on the right in the jury box. On the Bench, the Judge, calm, cold and serious and on the left was the witness-box in which we were to give on oath the evidence which might send him to his last home. The scene was most impressive and one never to be forgotten.

Mr. Griffiths addressed the jury for the Prosecution giving in detail the facts. He said that the prisoner was a married man whose wife and children were living at Exeter. In October, 1909, he went to live in Stalybridge, in which town he was employed as a carter. He later became acquainted with the woman whom he was charged with murdering and seemed to have been keeping company with her for some months. The facts were really very simple.

On Saturday, 21st May, Derrick was seen by a lodger

named Cook to be writing a letter at the table of his lodging-house and at 6.30pm he went with Cook and another lodger, Reynolds, for a walk. Whilst they were walking, Derrick began to play with three laces to which a swivel was attached. Reynolds asked him what he was doing to which he replied that he was making a rein for the horse.

At a place called the "Twin Bridge", Derrick left his companions saying he had a nail in his boot and went home again to the lodging-house. At 9.40pm, the prisoner and deceased were seen together by a man named Holloway and his wife, who said to Etchells "I have seen you now" and she replied "Yes, you have seen me many a time". Holloway said "Yes, I have", bade them goodnight and passed on. That was the last time the woman was seen alive.

At 11.10pm two men taking a walk near the quarry on Ridgehill heard groans, and on going to ascertain what it was, discovered a woman lying face downwards and a man rolling about the ground. They at once informed the police. A doctor was sent for and the man was taken to the Infirmary. The doctor found the woman was dead; her neck and face were swollen and livid and her tongue protruding from her mouth. She was taken to the mortuary.

Papers were found on the prisoner which would be put in as evidence; a lace had also been found near the spot covered with hair. The doctor had made a postmortem and found that death was the result of strangulation, and that the marks on the woman's neck could not have been self-inflicted. It was not essential to prove a motive in this case. He thought that when the jury had heard the evidence they would have no hesitation in saying that Derrick was guilty of the crime.

An objection was raised by Mr. Nelson (Derrick's Barrister) as to the letters being evidence and maintained that there was no proof that Derrick wrote them, and that the only evidence that it was the prisoner's handwriting would be that of a police officer. The Judge replied that if it was found not to be proved, the jury would reject the evidence, and so over-ruled the Barrister's objection.

Cook was then called who related the incident which took place during their walk. He was cross examined by Mr. Nelson who however, could not shake his evidence. Her mother was called who stated that on the 21st May, about 7.45pm, Derrick came to their house and asked for her daughter, and she had seen them together previously. Holloway was called and related the conversation that took place between them when they met in the fields that night; also, the men who made the discovery and informed the police.

Inspector Gee related how he found the body of the woman apparently dead, and the man groaning and bleeding from a wound in the throat. That he examined the prisoner's pockets and found letters and photos which tended to prove his guilt, and that he subsequently charged him with the crime to which he made no reply.

I then related that I was in charge of him at the Infirmary, and saw him write letters which I kept, and sent copies. His counsel here objected to my evidence, contending that a police officer was not the proper person to prove handwriting. The Judge disagreed with him and said that anyone could see there was but one handwriting. Mr. Nelson then said that I had secured the letters by means of a "trap". Mr. Griffiths said that such a word should not have been used and asked me to state how the writing came about.

I stated that the prisoner's employer came up to see him with reference to what he wished him to do, that he could not speak, and that we could not understand what he tried to say. That he made a motion with his hand as if he wanted to write. That I asked him and he nodded his head. That I handed him my pocket-book and he wrote what he wished to say in it. Mr. Nelson asked me if I had ever given expert evidence before in handwriting, and I replied that I was not an expert in such matters. The letters found upon him on the night of the tragedy and those I had secured were read, and evidence given as to the laces found near the spot.

The doctor then described the scene, the position of the body, the bruises and the cause of death. He was closely cross-examined by Mr. Nelson but he maintained his position throughout.

Derrick was then put in the box and denied his guilt, but he was severely cross-examined by the Prosecuting counsel, and from the keen questions asked and the evasive answers given, it was quite clear that his doom was sealed.

Mr. Ellis Griffiths then addressed the Jury and said that everything had been unquestionably proved, that there was only one possible verdict, and that would be that the woman met her death at the hands of the prisoner.

Derrick's counsel made an eloquent appeal on his behalf which lasted 40 minutes. He submitted that the Prosecution had failed to prove their case, that the prisoner had told them a straightforward and feasible story, and he prayed that God would guide the Jury right in the decision they came to. At the close of his speech there was slight applause which was at once suppressed.

The Judge's summing up was followed with rapt attention. He said the question the Jury had to decide was whether it was possible for the woman to have taken her own life. The medical evidence was perfectly clear and showed that she had not done so. The letters put in as evidence were undoubtedly written by the prisoner and in his opinion the case was quite clear. If the Jury believed Derrick's story, then they must acquit him; if they did not believe him, then there seemed no other course but to bring in a verdict of guilty.

The Jury retired at 4.45pm and were absent until 5.40pm. When they returned to the court, there was great excitement. The Clerk said: "Gentlemen, have you agreed upon a your verdict".

Foreman: "We have".

Clerk: "Do you find the prisoner at the bar guilty or not guilty of murder?"

Foreman: "Guilty".

"Sentence of Death".

Deathly silence then followed, the prisoner standing erect in front of the dock. On the black cap being placed upon the Judge's head, he betrayed distinct signs of emotion, his voice quavered somewhat, and tears visibly rolled down his cheeks.

Addressing the prisoner, he said: "Alfred Ernest Derrick, you have been found guilty by the Jury of the crime of wilful murder. For that crime, there is but one sentence known to the law. It is not my sentence. I have to declare to you the sentence which the law enacts for the crime of which you have been found guilty. That sentence is that you will be taken from whence you came, then to a place of execution, there to hang by the neck until you are dead, and your body buried within the precincts of the prison in which you were last confined. May the Lord have mercy on your soul".

The prisoner made no sign of concern. The warders closed up around him to prevent a collapse. Then a warder touched him on the shoulder and beckoned him towards the staircase leading down to the cells. He turned sharply round, then halted, and responding to the call of the warder slowly walked down the steps to the cells below. All eyes were turned upon him as he took a last glance around at the Court and people, and then he passed away from view of the outer world for ever.

At a later date, the sentence of death was commuted to one of penal servitude for life, and so we leave him to the tender mercy of his gaolers and his lonely prison cell, to bear the monotonous routine of his daily life and to repent and feel the remorse of one who has ever committed the awful crime of murder.